THE CALL OF THE SHAMANS

NORTHWATER

CONSTANTINE ISSIGHOS

Copyright 2013 © Constantine Issighos. Published in Canada. Printed in U.S.A. No part of this book may be reproduced or transmitted in any form or by any means, electronic or mechanical, including photocopying, recording, and/or by any information storage and retrieval system except by a reviewer who may quote brief passages in a review to be printed in a magazine, newspaper, or on the web without written permission in writing from the author/publisher. For information, please contact www.awaqkunabooks.com

NorthWater is an imprint of Awaqkuna Books Inc.

Vol. 16 Of THE AMAZON EXPLORATION SERIES:
THE CALL OF THE SHAMANS

Library and Archives Canada

ISBN 978-0-9878601-5-6

Library and Archives Canada Cataloguing in Publication

ATTENTION CHILDRENS ASSOCIATIONS, BOOK STORES, PUBLIC OR PRIVATE LIBRARIES: quantity discounts are available on bulk purchases of this book series.

THE AMAZON EXPLORATION SERIES
Children's Books
by
Constantine Issighos

1. Upper Amazon Voyage by River Boat
2. The People of the River
3. The Children of the River
4. Amazon's Nature of Things
5. Echoes of Nature: a Beautiful Wild Habitat
6. The Amazon Rainforest
7. Amazonian Sisterhood
8. Amazon River Wolves
9. Amazonian Landscapes and Sunsets
10. Amazonian Canopy: the Roof of the World's Rainforest
11. Amazonian Tribes: a World of Difference
12. Birds and Butterflies of the Amazon
13. The Great Wonders of the Amazon
14. The Jaguar People
15. The Fresh Water Giants
16. The Call of the Shamans
17. Indigenous Families: Life in Harmony with Nature
18. Amazon in Peril
19. Giant Tarantulas and Centipes
20. Amazon Ethnobotanical Garden
21. Amazon Tribal Warrios

The purpose of my journey deep into the heart of the Upper Amazon rainforest was to meet authentic shamans, to learn about their way of entering other dimensions, to see how they perform medicinal healings and how they communicate with the animal and the spirit world. As an indigenous cultural heritage, shamanism and traditional medicinal healing is still valued and respected today as it was by tribal ancestors. As a religious system, shamanism is marked by the belief that specific persons—men or women—have the ability to directly communicate with the spiritual world. The physical nature of the shaman's body serves as the means the spirits use to transmit their power into the human world.

The possession of the shaman by the spirits is an essential requirement of shamanism. The shaman's body is used as a medium for the spirits to channel their healing powers. This kind of belief was present and shared by many ancient societies, and can be found in the Mayan, Aztec, Islamic, Greek and Egyptian cultures. The magi-healers used various hallucinogens to induce a trance with dancing and chanting in order to help harness the powers of gods or spirits. Believing shaman's power is not an isolated characteristic of the Amazonian indigenous culture, nor does it constitute an exclusive esoteric domain of the shamans themselves. The shamanic mentality is spread throughout many communities, though their members may participate at different levels and in different degrees.

Two core essences appear to characterize the indigenous cultural shamanic tradition. The first is based on a fundamental belief in the existence of "mystical essences," or spiritual channels that must be acquired or possessed by the shaman to exorcise the threats to life and limb to which humans are prey. The ability to possess a mystical essence is the mark of a shaman having come of age. The virtue of the shaman resides in his ability to control these spirits in processes related to health and curing of illnesses. In this context, the shaman is able to acquired, preserved and multiply the spirits under his power.

The second core essence is to the apparent ability of members of communities to operate within two different states of "consciousness" or dualism. The ability to gain access to two different states of reality-- the physical and the spiritual-- refers to the "altered state of consciousness" necessary to carry on with daily life. The dual nature of physical reality and consciousness provides its own logic, and only by accepting this logic can one get beyond the superficial image of the shaman who sees spirits everywhere and who is unable to comprehend the laws of physics, presumably because of his mystical vision of reality. By understanding the dual nature of these indigenous people, an outsider can understand the great shamanistic tradition of the Amazon people. Thus the Amazon shaman is both respected and feared because of his ability to manipulate spirits in order to heal or to do harm. Because of his presumed powers to control the essence of mystical substances and his ability to establish connections among different worlds, he is perceived as the enforcing power behind various taboos, such as prohibitions against sexual relations and the eating of particular foods. The people fear him, for a powerful shaman can do harm with a single look.

Shamanism is thus one of the oldest spiritual pathways. It has neither laws nor temples; it is simply a spiritual journey into the "Other Reality" and the encountering of Spirits without any intermediaries. For millennia, spiritual journeys undertaken by shaman were perceived as real quests, an ancient way in which natural medicine, magic and mysticism were inextricably merged. To the eyes of a legitimate shaman, illness and pain are journeys into the forest, where the ill person is a lost soul, but can return, and the shaman is the seeker of the lost soul.

The shamanic way of healing is thus homeopathic, for shamans make no distinction between mind, body and spiritual illness. The shaman looks into the deeper layers of illness, a twilight zone where the physical, biological or psychic laws do not exist. Since the method is holistic, the shaman's healing way is regarded as extremely powerful.

There are plants throughout the Amazonian rainforest that traditional indigenous communities have used to heal, worship, and enter the world of the spirits. The sol purpose of these plants is to alter consciousness by being brewed into psychoactive drinks that bring visions and allow one to communicate with the invisible. Christian-based religions in Peru and Brazil also use psychoactive drinks as sacrament. People report visions of Jaguars, of turning into Eagles, of separating from their bodies, and of being able to travel through time and space.

In the Upper Amazon region, certain plants are believed to be living spirits—thus explaining the true origins of their healing functions. The vine Ayahuasca (Banisteriopsis caapi) is one of these plants. The term "ayahuasca" translates as "the vine of the soul." When consumed, it produces dramatic physical, mental and emotional changes. These changes are attributed to the living spirit of the plant—not to its ingredients. Among the residents and shamans in the Upper Amazon, ayahuasca holds honourable female qualities, and is often referred to as "Mother Ayahuasca" or "Grandmother Ayahuasca."

Another plant considered sacred is tobacco (Mapacho). Tobacco also played a central role in ceremonial activities of the native tribes of North America. First Nations people used tobacco to honour social bonds of friendship and to bind peace treaties between tribes. Ritual smoke blowing was a way native chiefs bestowed a blessing or protection against enemies. Mapacho is regarded as very sacred by Amazonian shamans who use it in combination with other plants in shamanic ceremonies. Tobacco leaf juice is often used as a source of hallucinogenic visions, and it is considered a medicine. Tobacco juice is also used in initiations, visionary quests, war preparations, victory feasts, and witchcraft and to induce vomiting. Even women partake of the juice in wedding feasts.

A mixture of Ayahuasca and Mapacho is considered very sacred by Amazonian shaman and medicine men and women. Medicine men process these plants for the general public and for shamanic practices. Mapacho juice is mixed with ayahuasca to produce a hallucinogenic drink. This drink is used exclusively in healing practices, for it is considered a shamanic medicine, not a health hazard, when used properly.

Many members of the Amazonian indigenous cultures take something into their bodies as a way of communicating with the spirits. These people are concerned about all indigenous cultures and plants that inhabit the rainforest. They are the bearers of knowledge that is vital to their survival and they are the keepers of medicinal plants that can be beneficial to all of humanity.

Every member of the Amazonian indigenous culture has learned something about how to care for their own mental, physical and spiritual health. They are as much a doctor as pharmacist. They have learned as much as they can about any medicinal remedies they utilize. This is part of the shamanic mentality, a common cultural phenomenon shared by the majority of the people in the Amazon rainforest.

Most western travelers in South America have heard something about the Ayahuasca medicinal plant and the insights that are experienced. Most are intrigued enough to consider trying it. What is absent from their understanding is that the Ayahuasca is absolutely not a recreational drug.

These western travelers are not part of the indigenous cultural shamanic mentality. Therefore, they are not ready to encounter the insight and workings of the Ayahuasca medicinal plant. They are ignorant of the fact that the Ayahuasca is essentially a medicine that works on all levels, physical, mental, emotional and spiritual. Its primary purpose is for healing an already ill person, not to give a trippy experience.

Purging is an essential part of the Ayahuasca healing process; you purge out all the negative traumatic experiences that have accumulated inside you over the years. That is what the Ayahuasca does best! The Ayahuasca healing process is very intense. It forces you to relive traumatic shadows from your past. Do not take this medicine lightly!

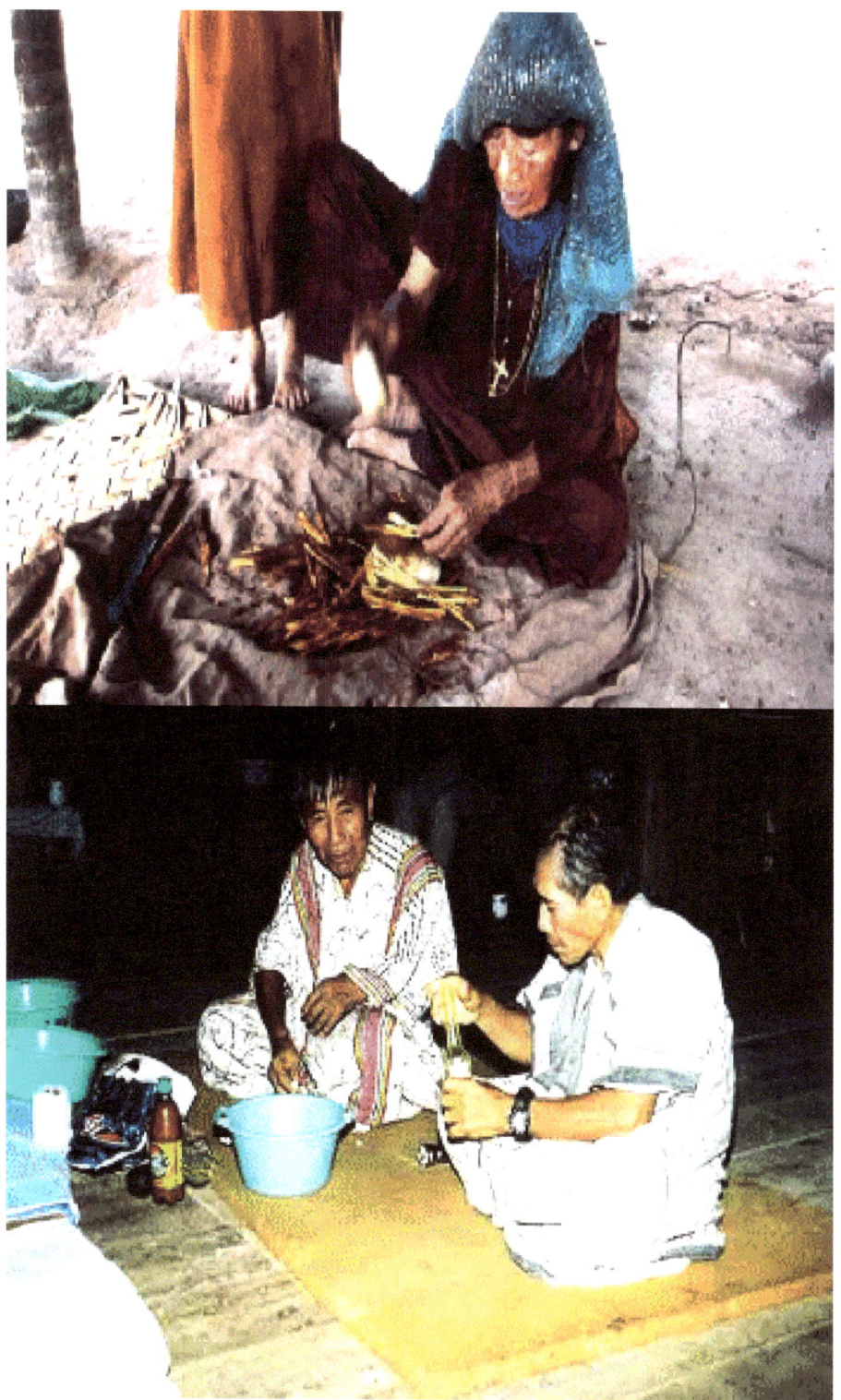

The Amazon Exploration Series — Constantine Issighos

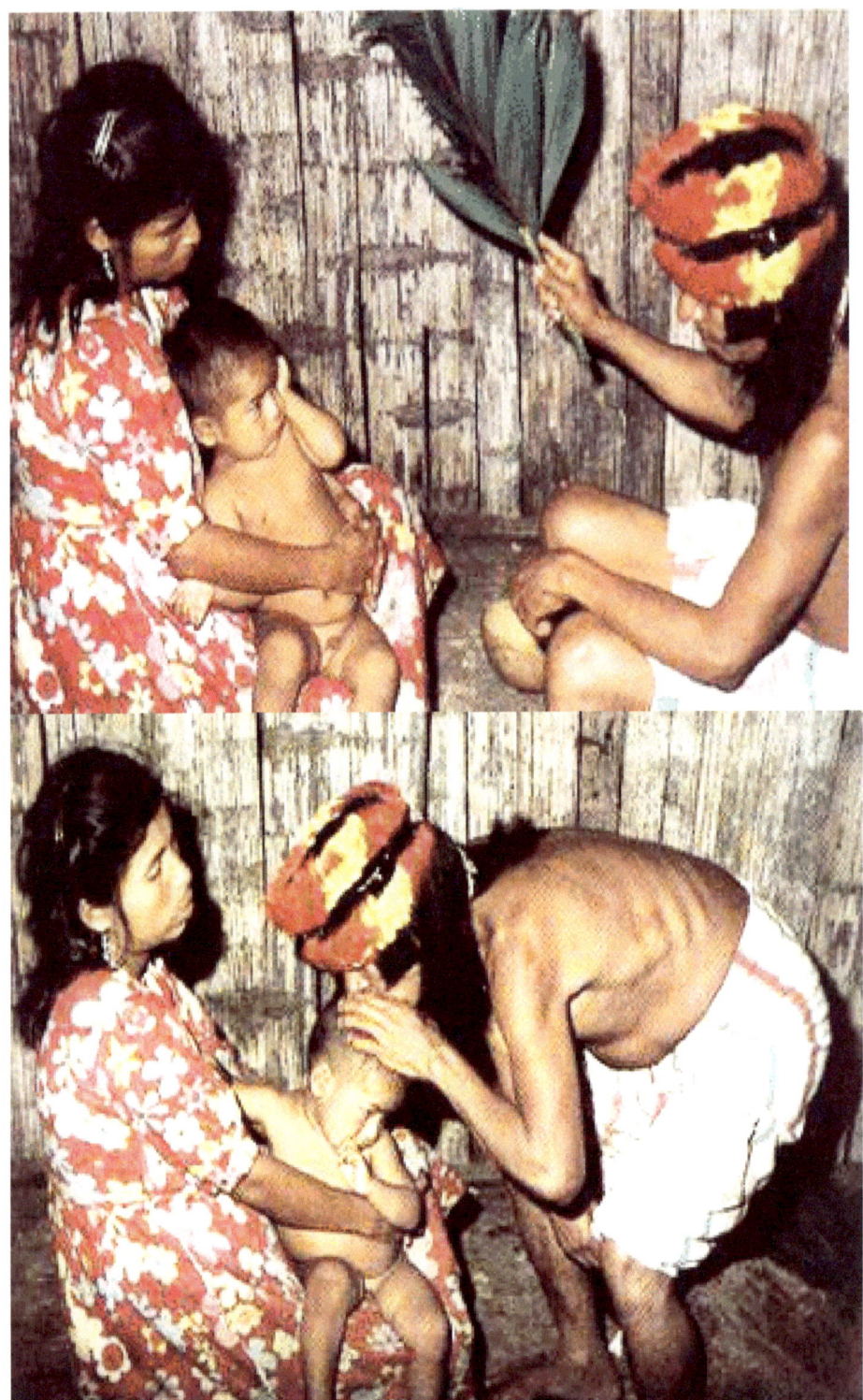

THE CALL OF THE SHAMANS

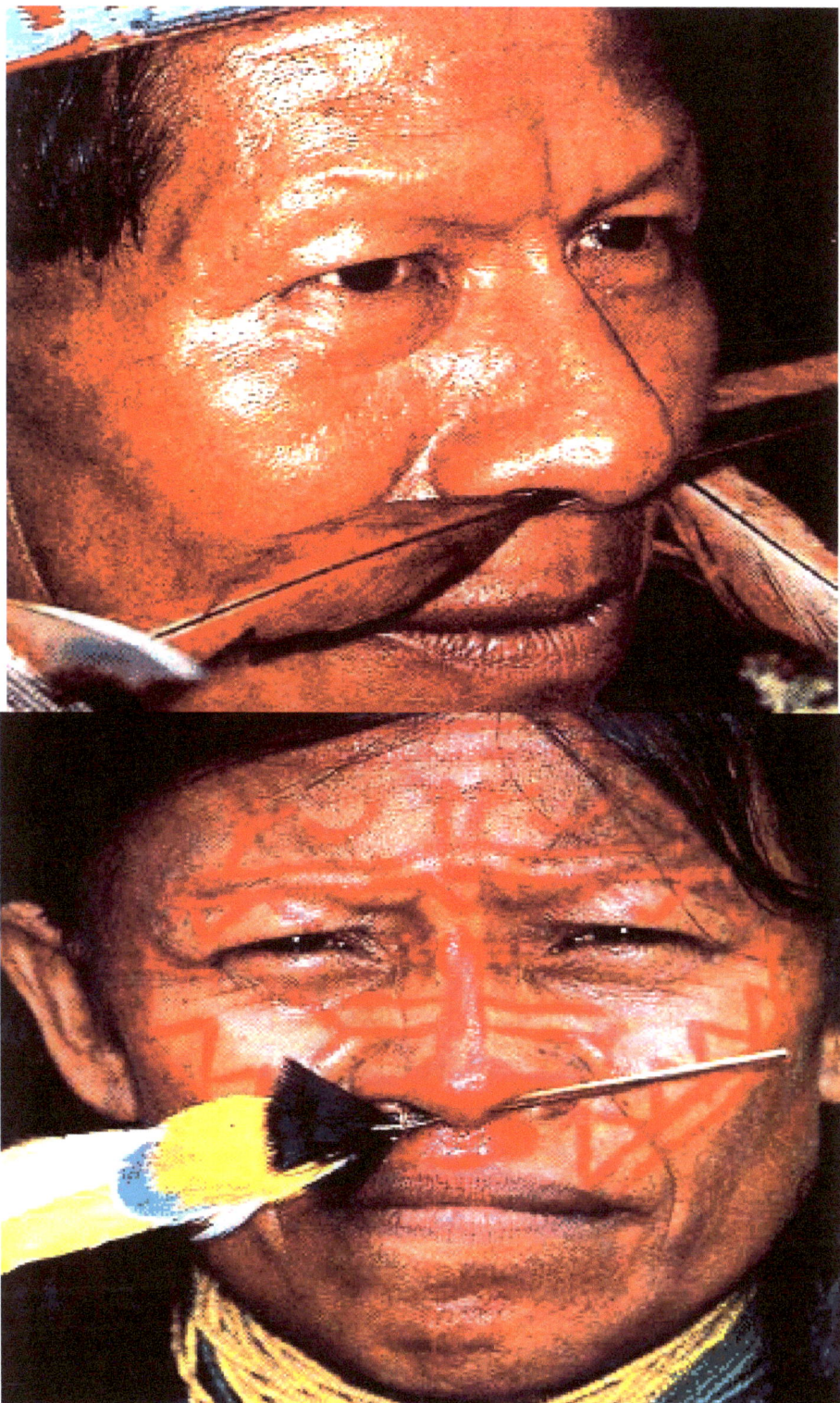

The Amazon Exploration Series   Constantine Issighos

The Amazon Exploration Series   Constantine Issighos

THE CALL OF THE SHAMANS   22

The Amazon Exploration Series   Constantine Issighos

THE CALL OF THE SHAMANS   24

Constantine Issighos   The Amazon Exploration Series

25   THE CALL OF THE SHAMANS

The Amazon Exploration Series — Constantine Issighos

THE CALL OF THE SHAMANS

The Amazon Exploration Series   Constantine Issighos

THE CALL OF THE SHAMANS

The Amazon Exploration Series   Constantine Issighos

THE CALL OF THE SHAMANS

The Amazon Exploration Series — Constantine Issighos

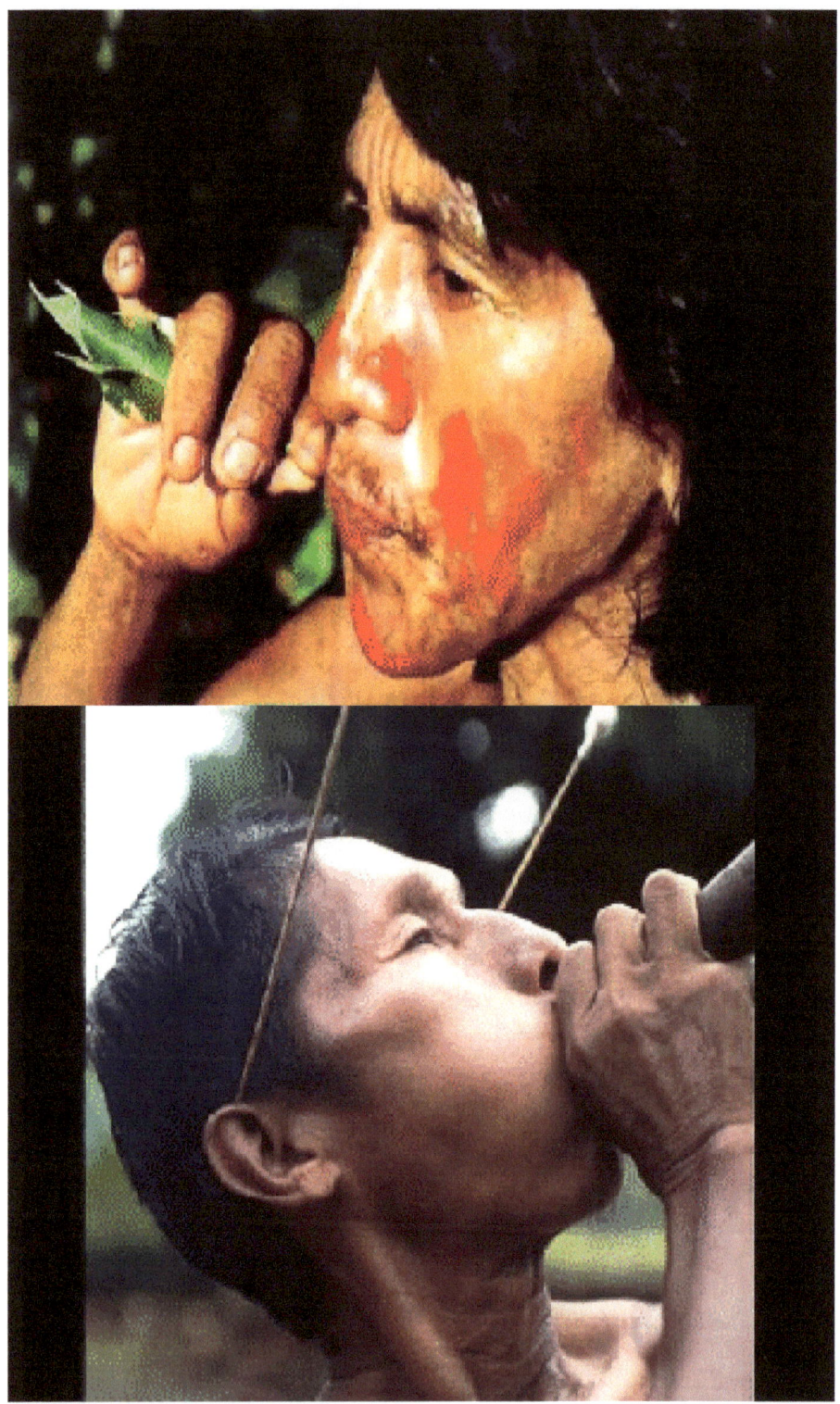

THE CALL OF THE SHAMANS

The Amazon Exploration Series — Constantine Issighos

THE CALL OF THE SHAMANS — 46

The Amazon Exploration Series — Constantine Issighos

THE CALL OF THE SHAMANS

www.ingramcontent.com/pod-product-compliance
Lightning Source LLC
Chambersburg PA
CBHW041754040426
42446CB00001B/25